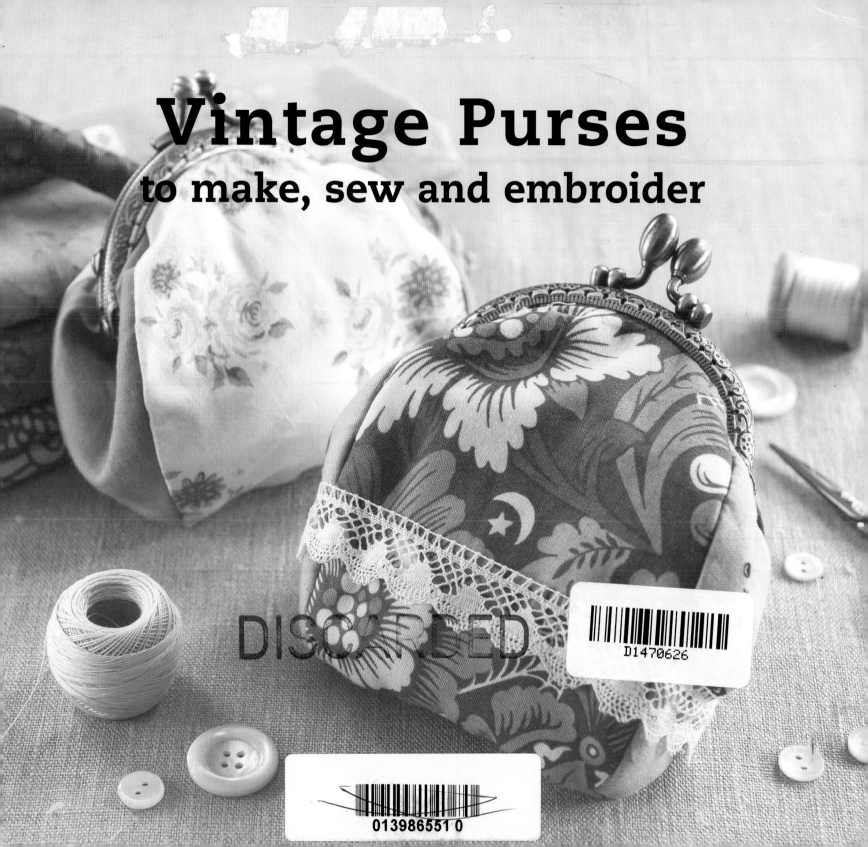

Vintage Purses
to make, sew and embroider

First published in Great Britain in 2014 by
Search Press Limited, Wellwood, North Farm Road,
Tunbridge Wells, Kent TN2 3DR

Original French title published as *Fermoirs Anciens
pour petits objets à coudre et broder*

Copyright © L'inédite, Paris, France 2013

English translation by Burravoe Translation Services

All rights reserved. No part of this book, text,
photographs or illustrations may be reproduced or
transmitted in any form or by any means by print,
photoprint, microfilm, microfiche, photocopier,
internet or in any way known or as yet unknown,
or stored in a retrieval system, without permission
obtained beforehand from Search Press.

ISBN: 978-1-78221-073-3

Designs: Sandrine Kielt-Michaud
Graphic Design: Géraud Lantuéjoul
Photography: Julien Clapot

Vintage Purses
to make, sew and embroider

Sandrine Kielt-Michaud

photography: Julien Clapot

Search Press

Contents

Projects

My sincere thanks to everyone who has encouraged and supported me throughout this project, especially the team at Inédite, my husband and my daughters.

I would also like to thank Westminster Fibers Inc for their wonderful 100% cotton fabrics, Free Spirit for their fun Nightshade range (PWTP106.VAPOR and PWT9017.VAPOR) and Toga for the adhesive fabrics used to make the Panther coin purse.

Introduction

Whenever I see vintage purses like these at craft shows, they remind me of the wonderful times I spent with my grandmother when I was young. To keep me entertained she taught me how to embroider bits of fabric, sew them into little bags and attach them to pretty purse frames.

This book is a chance for me to share and pass on to you my grandmother's skills.

I hope these little projects will give you as much pleasure as they have given me.

Sandrine Kielt-Michauld

Contact the author at:
lescreationsdesiriana@yahoo.fr
http://siriana.blog4ever.com
Facebook: Siriana Siriana

Tools and materials

Purse frames

You can buy purse frames over the internet, in craft shops, at craft shows and even at flea markets.

They come in a range of different sizes, shapes and colours (gold, silver etc).

Fabrics

You can use any kind of fabric you like to make these projects, but I mainly used cotton, laminated cotton, linen or felt.

- Thin wadding (batting)
- Cotton lining or cotton fabric that matches or complements your exterior fabric
- Fusible interfacing

And for a final decorative touch
- Charms, buttons, etc.
- Lace
- Ribbon
- Ribbon bows

Miscellaneous supplies
- Fabric glue
- Embroidery scissors, scissors, and pinking shears
- Quilting thread (stronger than ordinary thread when attaching purse frames) white waxed linen thread (which can be dyed with special fabric pens to match your fabrics), or coloured thread
- Embroidery thread
- Sewing thread
- Needles in different lengths: long and thin for sewing on purse frames, embroidery needles, hand-sewing needles and very long basting needles for tacking fabrics together

- Pins: useful for holding two pieces of fabric together ready for sewing and when checking the fabric is the right size for the frame
- Very small bulldog, binder or special fabric binding clips to hold the fabric in the frame while you are sewing it or waiting for the glue to dry

- Iron
- A sewing machine is useful, but not essential

For copying and transferring the templates and embroidery motifs
- Acetate film and a fine-tipped permanent marker pen suitable for use on plastic are useful for centring and targeting specific motifs on patterned fabric
- Non-permanent marker pens – a light colour for marking dark fabrics, a dark one for marking pale fabrics
- Tracing paper, tissue paper or greaseproof paper
- Tailor's chalk

Techniques and handy tips

Purse frames

Purse frames were first used as long ago as the 15th century, as proved by the discovery of an almoner's purse in Germany that was opened and closed by means of a metal purse frame.

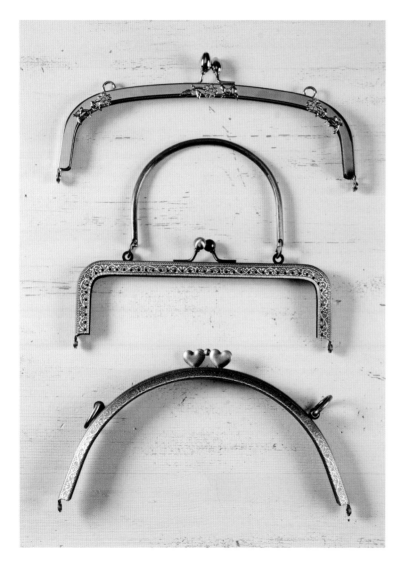

Metal purse frames have two 'arms' that comprise the two top sections of the frame, and two 'legs', one on either side. In the middle of the 'arms' are two small bobbles, which are twisted clockwise to open the purse and anti-clockwise to close it again. This type of purse frame first appeared in the second half of the 19th century, and is just right if you want to give your work a really vintage look. A purse frame can add not only strength but also a touch of class to your handbag, clutch bag, coin purse or carpet bag etc., and will make it easy to open and close. Purse frames come in a range of different colours, shapes and sizes.

You can also find what are known as flex frames, which make a distinctive 'popping' noise when they are opened and closed. Flex frames first became popular in the 1970s. Originally used for men's coin purses, these days they are often used for glasses cases too. Flex frames have two straight arms made from a rigid yet flexible material that are hinged together. The hinge on one side of the flex frame is held together by tiny pins. The flex frame opens when the hinges on both sides are squeezed together simultaneously, and closes again when the pressure is relaxed. The blue denim jeans purse (page 34) uses a flex frame.

Flex frames are also available in different lengths and widths. Projects using a flex frame need to have a hemmed channel left open on either side so that the flex frame can be fed through it.

Choosing the right purse frame

The project instructions show the dimensions of the frames I used to make each design, but these are for guidance only. You can adapt the finished size of your project to the size of your chosen frame.

It is important to buy your purse frame first, before you do anything else, because sizes can differ from one manufacturer to another – meaning there may be a few millimetres' difference in the height or width of the frame. Start by tracing the outline of the frame you are going to use on to a sheet of paper. Now copy it over (or lay it on top of) the templates you want to use and compare them. If your frame is slightly bigger, amend the template by making it slightly wider too. If it is smaller, make the template slightly narrower or make a couple of tiny tucks along the top of it until it approximates to the size you require.

Attaching your purse frame

As already explained in the previous section, there are several types of purse frame available, and the ways in which they are attached can differ.

When you open up the purse frame, you will find that most of them have a small U-shaped channel into which the fabric body is inserted before being securely attached.

Above left: sew-in and glued purse frame, no U-channel
Above right: sew-in purse frame with U-channel

Purse frames for gluing

Some purse frames are designed for the fabric to be glued into the U-channel with either a strong fabric glue or a universal glue suitable for use on both fabric and metal. To prevent the glue from staining the fabric do not apply too much; instead, dab it in tiny drops along the U-channel with a cocktail stick, then spread it evenly from edge to edge. As soon as the glue starts to dry, carefully push the fabric into the U-channel using a plastic or bone knitting needle or similar, then use a couple of small clips to hold the fabric firmly inside the U-channel until the glue is completely dry.

Other types of purse frame involve the fabric being both glued and sewn and these do not have a U-channel, although the technique required is similar to the one described above.

NB: Make sure the glue does not seep through the little sewing holes drilled along the purse frame.

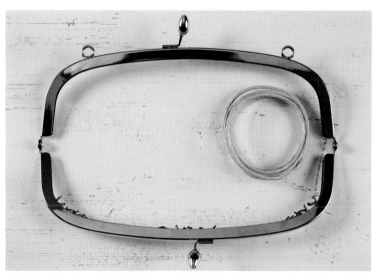

Glue-in purse frame

Purse frame for sewing and gluing
– the stitching line will show on the outside.

Sew-in purse frames

Use a quilting or other heavy duty thread when sewing fabric on to the frame, because the edges of the metal holes are sharp and ordinary sewing thread will soon break when it is being pulled through. Linen thread is even better, but whichever one you use, cut a fairly short length and use a needle thin enough to pass through the holes. You will need to open the purse frame out when you are sewing the fabric on to it.

Start by finding the centre of your fabric, which you can do by folding it in half and creasing it with your thumbnail, then clip it securely to the middle of the purse frame. Make a small knot in the end of your thread, insert the needle from the wrong side of the fabric and bring it up to the front through a hole in the centre of the frame. Working from the centre to the left or right as you prefer, push the needle down through the next hole,

Sew-in purse frame – the stitching line will show on the outside

then back out again through the next one along. Backstitch will provide a strong stitching line. Continue weaving in and out of the holes until you reach the end of the frame, then take a couple of tiny backstitches in the lining to secure the stitching line and cut off the excess thread.

Start again from the middle of the frame and complete the other side in the same way.

If you are using a lining and do not want the stitching line to show inside the purse, pass the thread between the exterior fabric and the lining as you work. Bring the needle out in the lining, push it back up through the same hole and out into the exterior fabric, then down again in the next hole along on the front of the purse frame, continuing this way to the end of the frame.

You can also disguise your stitches with lace, ribbon, beads etc.

If you only have white thread but want the colour of your thread to match your fabric, dye or colour it with a waterproof ink or a waterproof fabric pen.

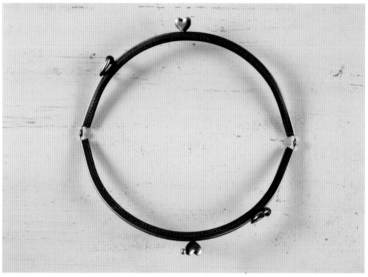

Sew-in frame – the stitching line wil show on the inside

Order of work

- Copy the template on to a sheet of Bristol board, acetate film or tissue paper. Rhodoid is a kind of transparent plastic that is also useful for making templates and can be centred over targeted motifs on patterned fabrics.

- Transfer all of the other pattern information from the templates on to your sheet of paper.

- Pin the template paper on to the fabric, paying attention to the grain line.

- Use special marking pencils that are available for copying outlines on to fabric. Once the motif has been traced, it can be transferred directly on to the fabric. The outlines will disappear when the fabric is washed.

- Copy the outline of your template, symbols and additional sewing information on to the exterior fabric, lining, wadding (batting) and fusible interfacing, using a wash-out fabric marker or tailor's chalk.

- Cut out the number of pieces shown. If the seam allowance is not already included, add 5mm (¼in) all around unless otherwise indicated. You will usually need to cut two pieces from the exterior fabric and two pieces from the lining fabric.

- To prevent the fabric from fraying, either use pinking shears or loosely overcast the edges.

- If you need to use fusible interfacing or wadding (batting), use a hot iron to attach it to the lining fabric.

- Double-sided fusible interfacing allows the wadding (batting) and the lining to be joined together. It has a rough (glued) side, which is applied to the wrong side of the pieces to be fused. To fuse, insert a piece of greaseproof paper between the fabric and the sole plate of a hot iron, press down and hold for a few seconds. Peel the greaseproof paper away from the fusible interfacing, carefully position the second piece of fabric on top and press down again with a hot iron. The two pieces are now fused together.

- Use a basting thread to tack two pieces of fabric right sides together all around the edge, leaving an opening between the marks indicated on the template for the purse frame. This opening allows you to pull your fabric through to the right side.

- If the pieces have a rounded edge, after they have been sewn together, make a series of very small V-shaped notches in the seam allowance, taking care not to snip across the seam line. This will help to keep the curve line smooth when the work is turned right side out.

- Once the pieces have been sewn together, check they will fit into the purse frame properly, using a couple of clips to hold the fabric in the purse frame. This is the time to make any adjustments needed to the exterior fabric, lining or wadding (batting).

- Stitch everything together along the tacked line. Remove your tacking stitches.

- Attach the fabric to the purse frame (see above). Depending on your frame, you will either need to sew the purse on to the purse frame or else glue it on. Some purse frames involve both gluing and sewing. Remember to use a short length of heavy-duty thread only, otherwise it could fray from being constantly rubbed against the metal holes and break.

Embroidery stitches

Most of the designs shown have been embroidered with two strands of embroidery thread. Try to keep your stitches as neat and even as possible. You may find it easier to use a small embroidery hoop to keep the fabric taut.

Running stitch

- Insert the needle at A, bring it back up at B, re-insert it at C, bring it back up at D, and continue in the same way.

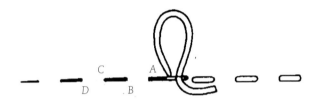

Lazy daisy stitch

- Bring the needle up the front of the fabric at A, make a small loop, then push the needle back down at A through the same hole, holding the thread down with the thumb of your other hand.
- Bring the needle back out at B, passing the thread underneath it in the middle of the loop then re-insert it at C just the other side of the loop to anchor the stitch to the fabric, 1mm from B.

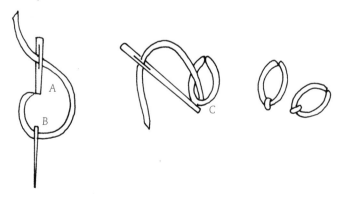

Backstitch

- Bring the needle up to the front of the fabric at B, stitch back to A, bring the needle back up at C, make another backstitch by inserting the needle at B, and continue in the same way.

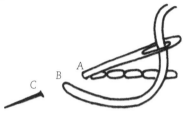

Chain stitch

- Bring the needle up to the front of the fabric at A, make a small loop, then push the needle back down at A, through the same hole. Bring the needle back out at B, passing the thread underneath it in the middle of the loop. Insert the needle at B and continue in the same way.

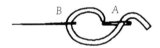

Satin stitch

- This involves making a series of flat, even stitches in which the thread is carried across the space to be filled and returned back underneath the fabric to the starting point.

French knot

- Bring the needle out at A and wrap your thread 2 or 3 times around it pulling the thread until it is nearly tight on the needle and holding the remaining length of thread firmly with your other hand. Re-insert the needle at A and gently tug the lead thread to tighten the knot.

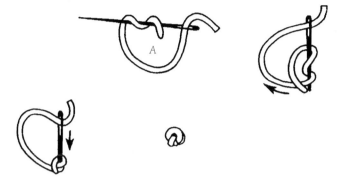

Couching

- Bring the six strands of foundation thread up at A and down again at B.
- Bring the two strands of couching thread up at C, reinsert the needle at D, and continue in the same way.

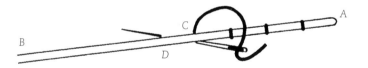

Buttonhole wheel

- Trace a circle and mark the centre B.
- Bring the thread up to the front of the fabric at A, push it back down at B, bring it back up at C and make a stitch, passing the thread under the needle.

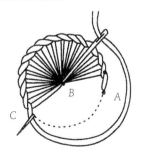

Roma scrunchie box

Dimensions: 16 x 16.5cm (6¼in x 6½in)

Materials
- Purse frame: 12.5 x 5cm (5in x 2in)
- Exterior fabric: 50 x 30cm (19¾ x 11¾in) for the box + 1 circle 9cm (3½in) in diameter for the bottom
- Lining fabric: 50cm x 30cm (19¾ x 11¾in)
- Lace: 40cm (16in)
- Polyester interfacing: 40 x 10.5cm (16 x 4in) + 1 circle 8cm (3¼in) in diameter

To make
Seam allowances are not included in this design, so please add 5mm (¼in) to the template when cutting out the exterior and lining fabrics. Note: cut the polyester interfacing on the marked line.

1 Copy template 1 on to the polyester interfacing and cut it out.

2 Draw an 8cm (3¼in) circle on to the polyester interfacing and cut it out. This will be used as the bottom of your box.

3 Form the sides of the box from the rectangle of polyester interfacing by sewing the two ends together in baseball stitch.

4 Complete the polyester interfacing box by sewing the 8cm (3¼in) circle of polyester interfacing to the sides using baseball stitch.

5 Join the upper and lower templates at points A and B, making one pattern piece, and trace it twice on to the exterior fabric and twice on to the lining fabric. Mark the points on the upper pieces where the purse frame will be attached (see pages 20–22).

6 Cut the two pieces from the exterior fabric and two from the lining fabric.

7 With right sides (RS) together, sew both sides of the two exterior fabric pieces up to the point marked 'purse frame' on the templates. Repeat with the lining fabric pieces.

8 With RS together, stitch the lining and the exterior fabrics together along the top edge (the one that will be inserted into the purse frame).

9 Turn right side out and make narrow tucks across the top as shown on the template (page 22). Anchor these down with a tiny stitch.

10 Sew across the bottom of the lining fabric.

11 Attach a gathering thread to the bottom edge of the lower exterior fabric.

12 Sew the purse frame to the upper piece.

13 Slip the polyester interfacing box between the lining and the exterior fabric (the lining will be inside the purse.

14 Gently pull the gathering thread to adjust the fabric to the circumference of the bottom of the purse.

15 The legs of the purse frame should rest on the top edge of the polyester interfacing pot. With the purse frame closed, gently tug the exterior fabric towards the bottom of the polyester interfacing pot. Insert a few pins to keep the fabric taut.

16 Slipstitch the bottom of the exterior fabric on to the polyester interfacing, remove the pins and securely stitch all around the base.

17 Sew the lace around your scrunchie box, as shown in the photograph.

Template for the lower half of the Roma scrunchie box

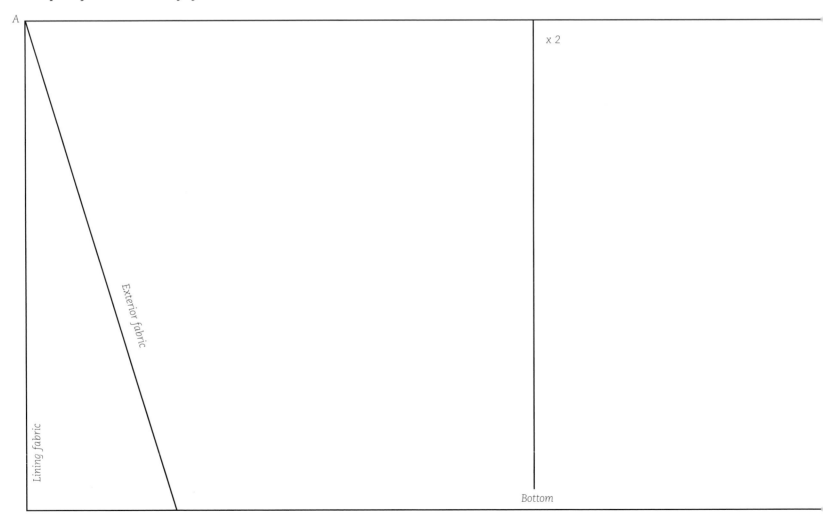

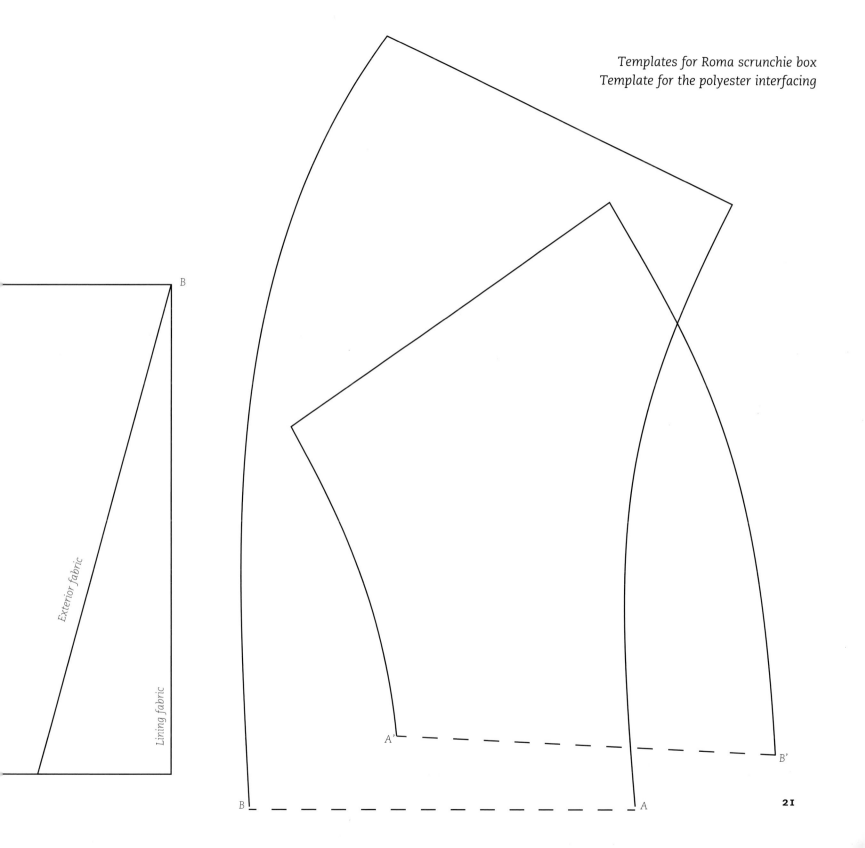

B

Exterior fabric

Lining fabric

A'

B'

B

A

Template for the upper half of the Roma scrunchie box

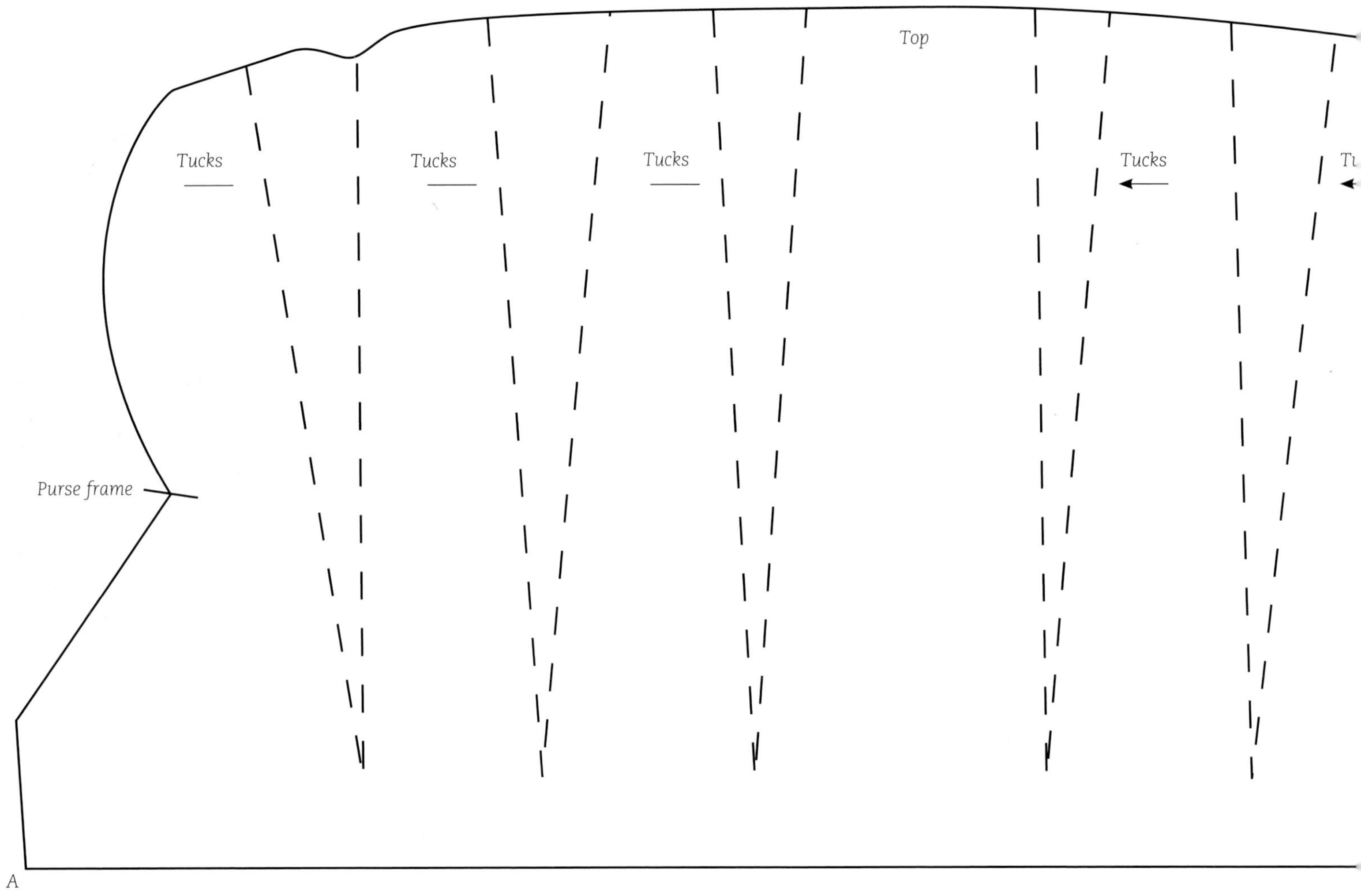

Top

Tucks

Tucks

Tucks

Tucks

Tu

Purse frame

A

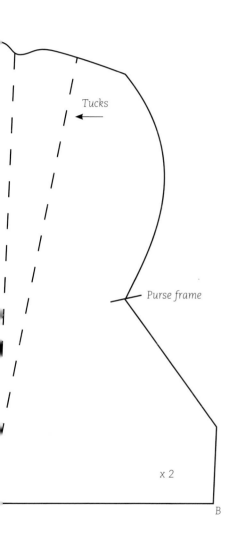

Tucks

Purse frame

x 2

B

Birdcage box

Materials

- Purse frame: 10 x 5.5cm (4 x 2¼in)
- Polyester interfacing: 28 x 8.5cm (11 x 3½in) + 1 circle 8cm (3¼in) in diameter (base)
- Lace: 60cm (24in)
- Floral fabric for cage door: 6 x 9cm (2¼ x 3½in)
- Plain pink exterior fabric: 32 x 11cm (12½ x 4¼in) + 1 circle 9cm (3½in) (base)
- Floral exterior fabric: 30 x 7cm (bottom half), (11¾ x 2¾in) (top half of cage)
- Lining fabric: 30 x 10cm (11¾ x 4in) + 30 x 7cm (11¾ x 2¾in) (top half of cage) + 1 circle 9cm (3½in) in diameter (base)
- Charms and decorations
- Embroidery thread
- Mini magnet for door (will be inserted under the exterior fabric and stitched in place)
- Very small metal button (door knob)

To make

1 Cut out the strip of polyester interfacing and the 8cm (3¼in) circle for the base of the cage.

2 Stitch the ends of the strip of polyester interfacing together using baseball stitch to form the circumference of the bird cage.

3 Attach the base to the circumference strip to form a pot shape.

4 Trace the template for the top half of the cage on to the floral fabric and lining (you need two of each). Seam allowances are included in this template.

5 Trace the vertical 'bars' of the cage on to the pink fabric for the lower half and the floral fabric for the upper half of the cage. The first 'bar' should be marked 2.5cm (1in) away from the edge and the rest at 2.5cm (1in) intervals. Embroider the 'bars' using the stitches suggested below:

1st line = couching
2nd line = lazy daisy stitch
3rd line = stem stitch
4th line = running stitch in a first colour with the spaces between filled with another row of running stitches in a second colour.
5th line = whipped running stitch: work a line of running stitches then, using another colour thread and starting at the first stitch, weave the needle under each stitch from the top. When you get to the end of the row, push the needle through the middle of the last stitch to bring it out on the back of the fabric, take a couple of stitches to anchor the thread and cut off the excess.

6 To attach the door: fold the rectangle of door fabric in half with RS facing, then sew around the edges leaving one side open. Turn through to the right side and stitch the opening closed. Attach the door to the pink fabric as shown in the photograph, using a wide spaced buttonhole stitch.

7 Attach the metal button in the middle of the right-hand side of the door.

8 Position the pink fabric of the cage for the lower half over the polyester interfacing pot, using clips to secure it at the top and pins around the bottom and up the side.

9 Take the 9cm (3½in) circle of plain pink fabric and turn the edge under to the wrong side all around. To maintain a neat circle, snip little notches all around the circle of fabric before hemming it. Neatly slipstitch the circle to the bottom of the cage.

10 Line up the mini door magnet underneath the pink fabric so that it is immediately opposite the metal door knob. Neatly sew around the magnet, stitching through the pink fabric and the polyester interfacing so that the magnet does not move. Handy tip: apply a drop of glue to the magnet (polyester interfacing side) to hold it in place while you are sewing.

11 To assemble the top of the bird cage, with right sides (RS) together, sew the floral fabric and lining together, leaving a small opening to turn the work through to the right side.

12 Sew the top half of the cage to the purse frame.

13 Attach the top half of the cage to the bottom half by sliding the floral fabric (top half) between the polyester interfacing and the pink fabric (bottom half). Sew the top half to the polyester interfacing.

14 Fold the lining fabric for the bottom half of the cage in half lengthways with RS together. Taking a 5mm (1¼in) seam, sew the short edges together, then press the seam open. With RS together, stitch this tube to the lining circle base. Tuck the lining down into the bottom of the cage, fold over the top part of the lining to make a narrow hem and neatly stitch it to the interior fabric used for the top half of the cage.

15 Sew the lace around the middle and the base of the cage as shown.

16 Attach the charms to the purse frame and the cage: you could also sew a small charm underneath the cage door.

Template for Birdcage box

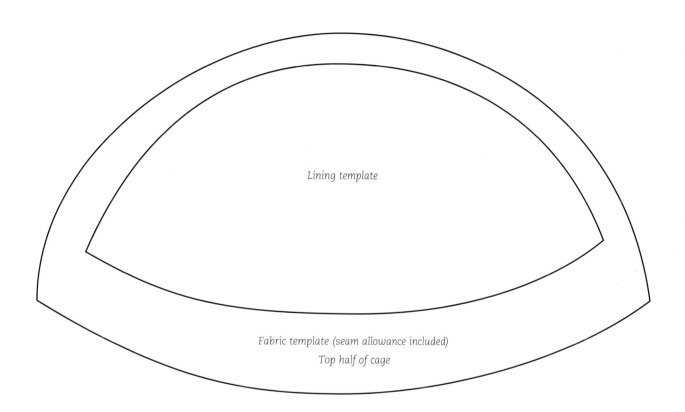

Lining template

Fabric template (seam allowance included)
Top half of cage

Rustic bread bag

Materials

- Laminated cotton fabric: two pieces each 35 x 75cm (13¾ x 29¼in)
- Purse frame with eyelets: 20 x 9cm (7¾ x 3½in)
- Lace (for handle): 50cm (19½in)
- Lace (for trim): 29cm (11½in)
- Contrast fabric or plain cotton on which to embroider the words Mon sac à pain (My Bread Bag): 28 x 9.5cm (11 x 3¾in)
- Stranded embroidery cotton: (here DMC shade no. 3782)

To make

1 Transfer the embroidery outlines to the plain or contrast fabric and complete as shown below. Attach the lace to the top edge of the embroidered panel and turn a small hem around the remaining three edges. Stitch the embroidered panel on to one of the pieces of fabric at an angle, right side uppermost.

2 Line up the tops and bottoms of two pieces of laminated cotton fabric with right sides (RS) facing.

3 To make the gusset of the bread bag, carefully line up the side stitching line with the gusset stitching line. When pressed flat it will form a triangle; sew across this 6cm (2¼in) from the tip.

4 Sew the laminated cotton fabric on to the purse frame.

5 Attach the lace handle by threading it through the eyelets on the frame, then fold it back on itself overlapping about 4cm (1½in) and stitch securely together.

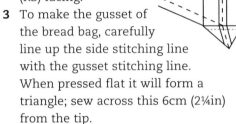

Pretty heart purse

Dimensions: 10 x 13cm (4 x 5in)

Materials

- 2 purse frames: each 5 x 3.5cm (2 x 1½in)
- Floral fabric: 26 x 14cm (10¼ x 5½in) (exterior)
- Plain fabric: 26 x 20cm (10¼ x 7¾in) (exterior)
- Lining fabric: about 26 x 24cm (10¼ x 9½in)
- Lace: 18cm (7in)
- Piping cord: 90cm (36in)
- 1 small bow

To make

1 Transfer the heart template on to the fabric, tracing the complete heart shape once (for the lining), and once divided into 2 parts (exterior of purse).

2 Cut two divided heart shapes from the floral and plain exterior fabrics and cut two whole heart shapes from the lining, adding a 5mm (¼in) seam allowance around the template.

3 With right sides (RS) together, stitch the floral and plain fabric pieces together by stitching along the broken line marked on the template. Place the two completed heart shapes RS together then stitch together between the marks shown for the purse frame.

4 Sew or glue the lace along the seam line and attach the bow.

5 With RS together, sew the two pieces of lining together between the points marked on the template for the purse frame. Leave wrong side (WS) out and stitch another line to separate the two halves of the interior following the broken line on the template. You will have two purse pockets that can be opened individually.

6 Tuck the lining into the exterior fabric with WS together.

7 Insert the top of the purse and lining pieces into the purse frames and stitch to secure.

8 Attach the piping cord for the purse strap.

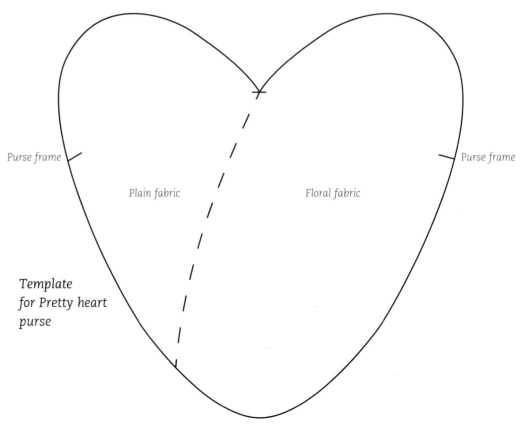

Purse frame

Purse frame

Plain fabric

Floral fabric

Template for Pretty heart purse

Kokeshi glasses case

Dimensions: 19 x 9cm (7½ x 3½in)

Materials

- Stranded embroidery cotton: black, red and pink beige
- Purse frame: 9 x 5cm (3½ x 2in)
- Zip: 12cm (4¾in)
- Flower charm
- For interior pouches: 3 pieces of plain fabric each 21 x 11cm (8¼ x 4¼in) (decorated with stamped ink motifs (shade Sand from Versacraft optional)
- Exterior fabric: 2 pieces of toning fabric in a light colour, each 21 x 11cm (8¼ x 4¼in)
- 1 small piece of pink beige cotton fabric (face)

Embroidery stitches

- Stem stitch (to outline kimono, eyes and mouth)
- French knot (inside the eye)
- Satin stitch (cheeks and hair)

To make

1 Trace your template on to your five pieces of fabric. This template includes a 5mm (¼in) seam allowance.

2 Stitch the face on to the right side of one of the exterior fabrics. Transfer the embroidery design and complete using the stitches indicated. Use one strand of embroidery cotton throughout, except for the hair, which is worked in two strands.

3 Stack the five layers of fabric in the following order: exterior fabric with right (embroidered) side uppermost, three pieces of lining fabric, the other piece of exterior fabric wrong-side up.

4 Insert the zip into the bottom of the purse where the template indicates, sewing it through three thicknesses of fabric on one side and two on the other (embroidered side).

5 At the point where the sections are attached to the purse frame, make a small narrow turning on each piece of fabric, layering them in the order shown below. Neatly oversew the sides together.

6 Insert the back and front sections into the purse frame.

Kokeshi layout

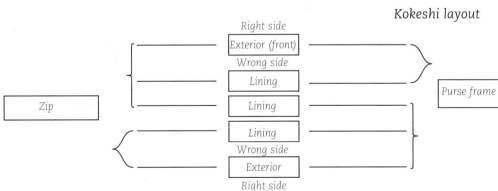

Embroidery outlines and templates for Kokeshi glasses case

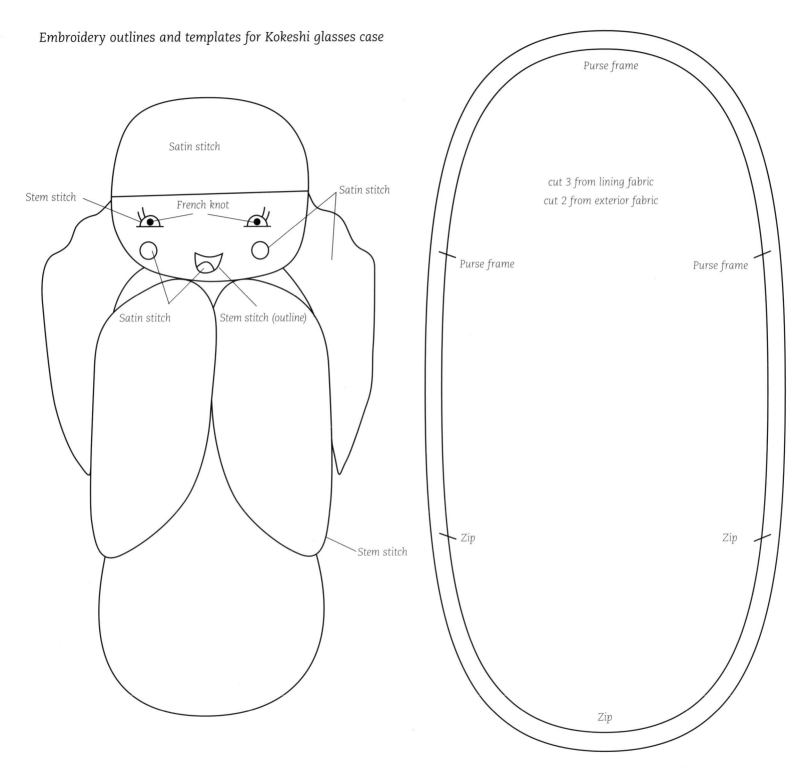

Satin stitch

Stem stitch

French knot

Satin stitch

Satin stitch

Stem stitch (outline)

Stem stitch

Purse frame

cut 3 from lining fabric
cut 2 from exterior fabric

Purse frame

Purse frame

Zip

Zip

Zip

Template for Blue demin jeans purse

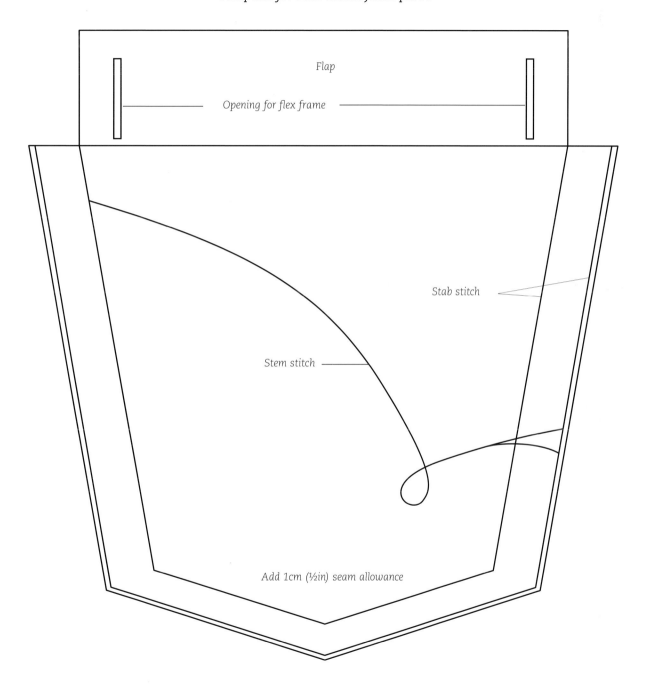

Flap

Opening for flex frame

Stab stitch

Stem stitch

Add 1cm (½in) seam allowance

Blue denim jeans purse

Materials
- 2 back pockets from a pair of denim jeans similar heavy duty fabric
- 2 strips of heavy-duty fabric for the flap: 13.5 x 3cm (5¼ x 1¼in)
- Lace: 32cm (12½in)
- Flex frame: 12cm (4¾in)
- Charms, length of fine chain, flowers
- 2 hinged rings and spring lever hooks for attaching the chain

To make
1 Cut the two back pockets off a pair of jeans leaving a 2cm (¾in) strip of jeans fabric all around. Trim away surplus fabric behind each pocket.

2 The flap must be wide enough to accommodate the flex frame.

Alternatively:
If the flap on the jeans pockets is already sufficiently wide, stitch it 2cm (¾in) down from the top edge, leaving both sides open for the flex frame.

3 If the pockets do not have a flap, attach a 13.5 x 3cm (5¼ x 1¼in) strip of heavy-duty fabric to each one. To do this, sew the top edge of the strip to the top edge of the pocket, right sides (RS) together. Turn the strip of fabric over towards the inside of the pocket.

Add a second stitching line along the strip about 2cm (¾in) below the first stitching line at the top of the RS of the pocket, leaving both sides open for the flex frame.

4 With RS of the pockets together, sew them together down one side, across the bottom, and up the other side.

5 Open the flex frame by removing the hinge pins with the tip of a sharp nail or similar. Slide the two arms of the flex frame through the openings.

6 Re-insert the hinge pins to close the flex frame.

7 Insert the hinged rings through the top half of the purse and attach the spring lever hooks for the hand chain and decorate both sides of your coin purse with charms.

8 Sew the lace across the RS top of the pocket.

Alternatively:

1 If you are not using jeans pockets, copy the template on page 35 twice on to a piece of heavy-duty fabric and cut these out along the outside line.

2 Complete the embroidery design in stem stitch.

3 Leave openings in the flap to insert the flex frame then sew the edges of the flaps to the inside of both pieces of fabric. Insert the flex frame, reinsert the hinge pins, and decorate.

Louane ladybird purse

Materials

- Laminated cotton fabric (red and white polka dot)
- Purse frame: 5 x 3.5cm (2 x 1½in)
- Flower and leaf charms
- Hinged ring for attaching charms

To make

1 Transfer the template on to the laminated cotton (the seam allowance is already included) and cut them out.

2 With right sides (RS) together, stitch the two pieces for the back of the ladybird together, starting in the middle and sewing to either end.

3 Stitch the back to the front (the 'belly'). Leave the top open, as it will be sewn on to the purse frame.

4 Attach the flowers and the leaf to the back of the purse using a hinged metal ring.

5 Sew the body of the purse on to the frame.

Template for Louane ladybird purse

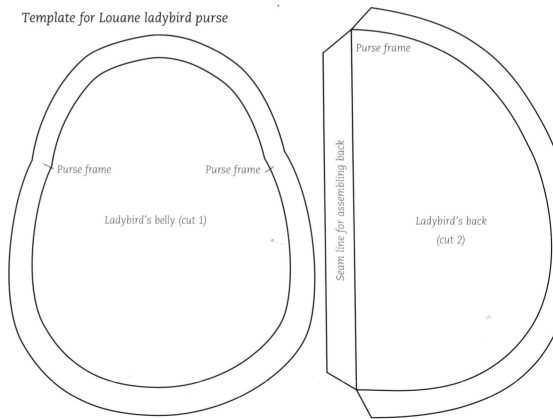

Purse frame

Purse frame

Ladybird's belly (cut 1)

Purse frame

Seam line for assembling back

Ladybird's back (cut 2)

Nostalgic jewellery box

Dimensions: 14 x 7cm (5½ x 2¾in)

Materials
- Rectangular purse frame: 12 x 4.5cm (4¾ x 1¾in)
- Exterior fabric: about 30 x 30cm (12 x 12in)
- Lining fabric: about 30 x 30cm (12 x 12in)
- Lace: 40cm (16in)
- Polyester interfacing: 20 x 20cm (8 x 8in)
- Double-sided fusible webbing: 10.5 x 4.5cm (4 x 1¾in)

To make
1. Transfer the template for the back/front and sides on to the exterior and lining fabrics and cut out. Important: no seam allowance is given, so please add 5mm (¼in) when cutting out the exterior and lining fabrics, but cut the polyester interfacing on the marked line.
2. Cut a back and a front piece from the exterior and lining fabrics and the polyester interfacing, and two in the same fabrics from the side template.
3. Cut one 14 x 9.5 cm (5½ x 3¼in) rectangle each from the exterior and the lining fabrics (box base). Do not forget to add a 1cm (½in) seam allowance on all sides.
4. Cut one 10.5 x 6.5cm (4½ x 2¼in) rectangle each from the exterior fabric and the lining for the box lid. Do not forget to add a 1cm (½in) seam allowance on all sides.
5. From polyester interfacing, cut one 14 x 9.5cm (5½ x 3¾) rectangle for the base and one 10.5 x 5.5cm (4¼ x 2¼in) rectangle for the lid.
6. Form the polyester interfacing into a box shape by sewing the sides, back and front to the base, using baseball stitch. Do not sew the lid on yet.
7. With RS together, sew the sides, back and front of the exterior fabric to the sides and back/front. Repeat for the lining. Turn the exterior fabric side right side out but leave the lining wrong side out.
8. Insert the polyester interfacing box between the exterior fabric and the lining.
9. To make the lid, sew the lining and exterior fabrics RS together, leaving one side open.
10. Turn the whole thing through to the right side. The purse frame will be attached above the sewn section.
11. Stitch the unsewn section of the lid lining to the interior lining of the box, RS together (rear section of the box).
12. Lay the fusible webbing on top of the polyester interfacing lid.
13. Slip the polyester interfacing lid between the lining and exterior fabric lids. The side with the fusible webbing should point towards the top of the lid. Position the polyester interfacing about 5mm (¼in) away from the sewing line, so that you can sew on the purse frame.

14 Press down on the top of the lid with a hot iron so that the fusible webbing bonds the polyester interfacing into position.

15 Sew the purse frame on to the fabric and the lining, but do not sew the polyester interfacing into the U-channel of the purse frame.

The lower end of the purse frame should be resting on top of the polyester interfacing box and the arms of the purse frame should be flush with the lid.

16 To hinge the box and lid together, slide the lid fabric (not sewn) between the back of the polyester interfacing box and the exterior fabric. Close the lid, insert a few pins to mark the sewing line, then neatly stitch together.

17 Decorate your box by sewing the lace trim flush with the top of the purse frame.

Templates for Nostalgic jewellery box

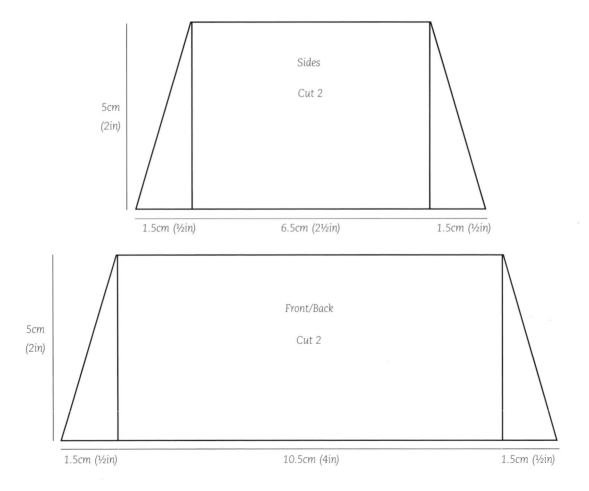

5cm (2in)

1.5cm (½in) 6.5cm (2½in) 1.5cm (½in)

Sides

Cut 2

5cm (2in)

1.5cm (½in) 10.5cm (4in) 1.5cm (½in)

Front/Back

Cut 2

Embroidery motifs for Great getaway sewing kit

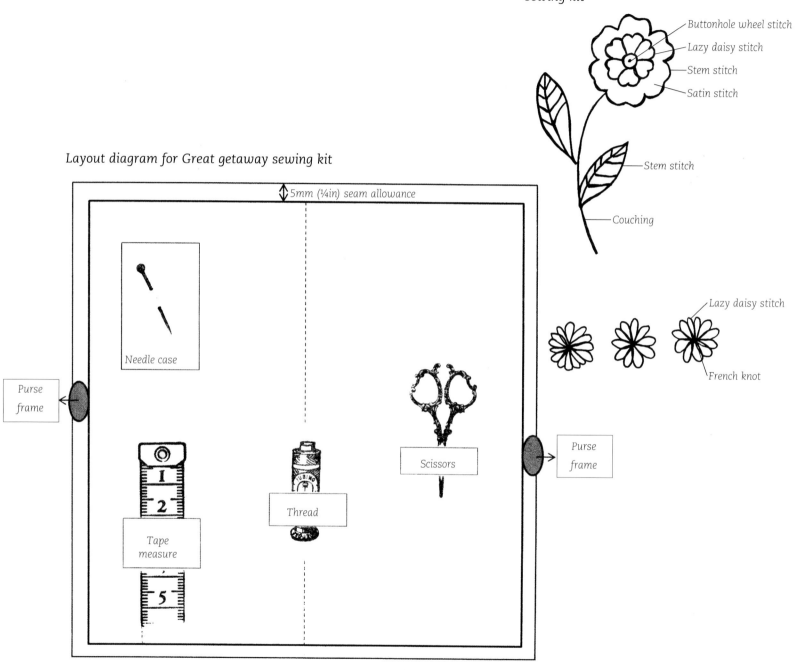

Buttonhole wheel stitch

Lazy daisy stitch

Stem stitch

Satin stitch

Stem stitch

Couching

Lazy daisy stitch

French knot

Layout diagram for Great getaway sewing kit

5mm (¼in) seam allowance

Needle case

Purse frame

Purse frame

Scissors

Tape measure

Thread

Great getaway sewing kit

Dimensions: 13 x 7cm (5 x 2¾in)

Materials
- Rectangular purse frame: 12.5 x 6.5cm (5 x 2½in)
- Exteroir fabric: 15 x 15cm (6 x 6in)
- Lining fabric: 15 x 15cm (6 x 6in)
- Medium or lightweight wadding (batting)
- Double-sided fusible webbing (optional:) 15 x 15cm (6 x 6in)
- Lace: 17cm (7in)

Inside the sewing kit
- Ribbon: 3 cm (1¼in)
- Lace: 18 cm (7in) fine lace for holding needle case closed + 15cm (6in) elasticated lace to hold spool of thread and tape measure.
- Embroidery floss to match your fabrics
- Soft felt: two pieces 2.5cm x 8cm (1 x 3¼in) for needle case

To make
Felt needle case

1 Lay the two pieces of felt on top of one another, mark the middle and stitch together from top to bottom. Cut the 18cm (7in) length of fine lace in half. Attach one piece at the edge and in the middle of the top layer of felt and one piece at the edge and in the middle of the bottom layer of felt so that it can be kept closed when not in use (see photograph). Sew a little motif on to the cover of the needle case or embroider the outline of a pin.

2 Sew the needle case in the position shown on the layout diagram (see page 43).

3 Sew on the ribbon to hold the scissors and the elasticated lace that will hold the spool of thread and the tape measure in the positions shown on the template.

4 Trace the flower motif on to the exterior fabric (see page 43) and embroider using the stitches shown.

5 Sew the lace just above the embroidered design, 5mm (¼in) from the edge of the fabric.
Handy tip: to prevent fraying, rather than cutting off the excess lace, fold it between the fabric and the lining.

6 Lay the wadding (or fix it with fusible webbing) on the wrong side (WS) of the lining fabric.

7 With right sides (RS) together, sew the exterior fabric and the lining (plus wadding) together, leaving an opening down one side so that it can be turned the right way out.

8 Turn through to the right side and slipstitch the opening closed.

9 Sew the purse on to the purse frame on both sides and finish by taking a few stitches to hold the fabric flush with the legs of the frame.

Primavera clutch purse

Materials
- Exterior fabric and lining: 30 x 15cm (12 x 6in) for each of front and back + 32 x 7cm (12½ x 2¾in) for gusset and sides
- Wadding (batting): 30 x 15cm (12 x 6in) + 32 x 7cm (12½ x 2¾in) for gusset and sides
- Lace: 60cm (24in)
- Purse frame: 13 x 5cm (5 x 2in)
- Embroidery threads in deep red, pink, white and green
- Brad fasteners

To make
1 Copy the templates twice on to the exterior fabric, lining and wadding. Handy tip: the wadding for the gusset can be folded in half and cut in a single piece. To do this, place the fold of the wadding on the broken line marked on the template.
2 Trace the embroidery motifs on to the exterior fabric (front, back and gusset)
3 Complete using the embroidery stitches shown. Insert small brad fasteners through the centres of the embroidered flowers.
4 Cut out your pieces of fabric.
5 With right sides (RS) together, stitch the two gusset pieces together into a single piece. Press the seam open. Repeat for the lining and wadding if you have not cut it out in a single piece.

6 Mark the centre of each piece, front and back, with a pin.
7 Embroidered fabric: pin the gusset to the front piece of the clutch purse RS together, carefully matching the centres marked with a pin. Starting from the centre, stitch to the point where the purse frame is inserted (see template). Complete the other side to match, then repeat for the back.
8 Cut the 60cm (24in) length of lace into four equal 15cm (6in) lengths. Sew two lengths at one end of the gusset piece (just below where the purse frame is inserted) and the other two lengths on the other side to match.
9 Assemble and sew the lining together as described in step 7 and also the wadding.
10 Turn the embroidered section of the coin purse RS out. Insert the wadding and then the lining, wrong sides (WS) out.
11 Fold under the edges of the sides and slipstitch them together.
12 Stitch everything together along the top edge, making sure that the lace does not catch in the sewing line; the sewing line will be hidden inside the U-channel of the purse frame.
13 Sew on the purse frame.
14 Tie the lace into bows on either side, as shown.

Embroidery motifs and templates for Primavera clutch purse

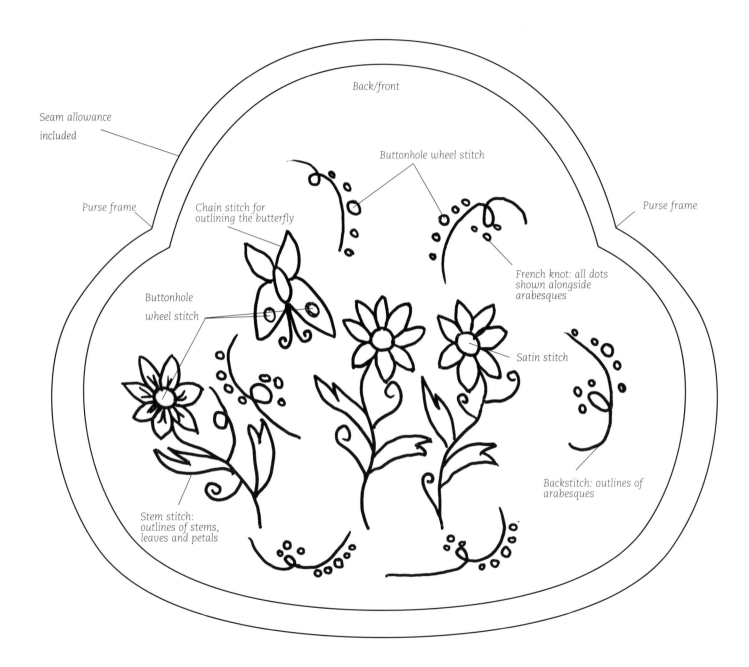

Back/front

Seam allowance included

Purse frame

Purse frame

Buttonhole wheel stitch

Chain stitch for outlining the butterfly

French knot: all dots shown alongside arabesques

Buttonhole wheel stitch

Satin stitch

Backstitch: outlines of arabesques

Stem stitch: outlines of stems, leaves and petals

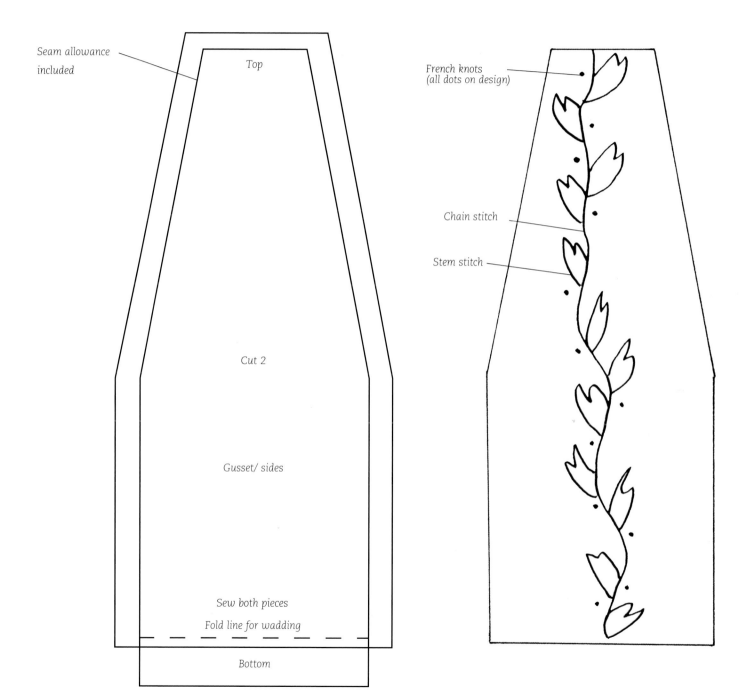

Seam allowance
included

Top

Cut 2

Gusset/ sides

Sew both pieces

Fold line for wadding

Bottom

French knots
(all dots on design)

Chain stitch

Stem stitch

Pretty coin purse

Dimensions: 12.5 x 12cm (5 x 4¾in)

Materials
- Plain cotton or linen: 30 x 40cm (12 x 15¾in)
- Lace: 26cm (10¼in)
- Purse frame: 8 x 4cm (3¼ x 1½in)
- Lining fabric 30 x 40cm (12 x 15¾in)
- Embroidery thread to match your fabric

To make
1. Trace the pattern piece on to the plain fabric and the lining. This includes a 5mm (¼in) seam allowance.
2. Transfer the embroidery motif on to the front piece of the purse and complete as shown on page 52.
3. Place the front and back right sides (RS) together, then sew the side seams together between the marks indicating the position of the purse frame. Repeat with the lining.
4. With RS together, stitch the gusset to the assembled front and back. Repeat for the lining.
5. Turn the body of the purse RS out then tuck the lining into it (leave this WS out).
6. Sew both fabrics together along the top. The sewing line will be hidden inside the U-channel of the purse frame.
7. Sew the purse on to the purse frame.
8. Stitch the lace flush with the purse frame on both sides.
9. The back can be embellished with ribbon or more lace.

Gusset 5.5 x 9.5cm (2¼ x 3¾in)

Embroidery motifs and template for Pretty coin purse

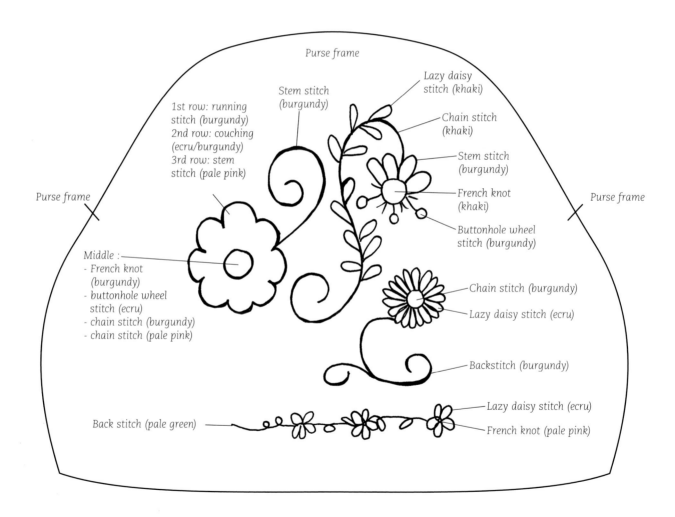

Purse frame

Stem stitch (burgundy)

Lazy daisy stitch (khaki)

Chain stitch (khaki)

Stem stitch (burgundy)

French knot (khaki)

Buttonhole wheel stitch (burgundy)

1st row: running stitch (burgundy)
2nd row: couching (ecru/burgundy)
3rd row: stem stitch (pale pink)

Purse frame

Purse frame

Middle :
- French knot (burgundy)
- buttonhole wheel stitch (ecru)
- chain stitch (burgundy)
- chain stitch (pale pink)

Chain stitch (burgundy)

Lazy daisy stitch (ecru)

Backstitch (burgundy)

Lazy daisy stitch (ecru)

Back stitch (pale green)

French knot (pale pink)

Template for Sicilia evening purse

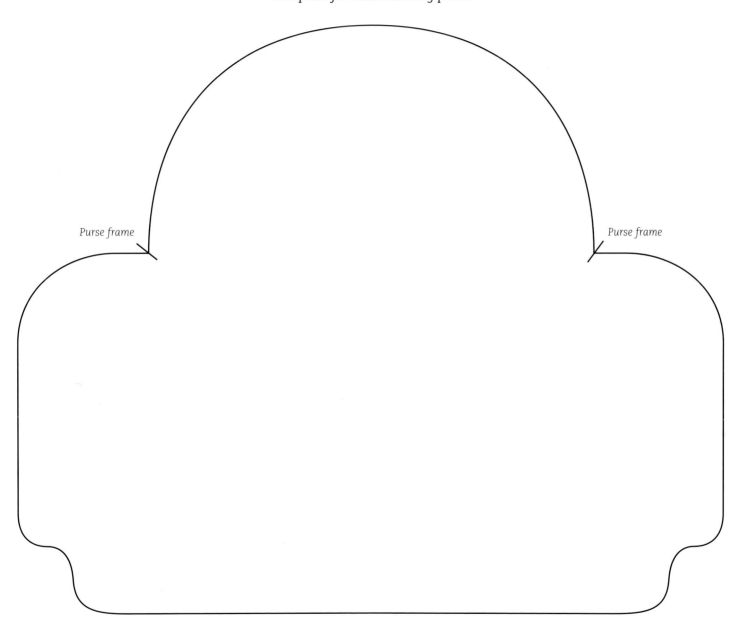

Purse frame

Purse frame

Sicilia evening purse

Dimensions: 18.5 x 14cm (7¼ x 5½in)

Materials
- Purse frame 12.5 x 7cm (5 x 2¾in)
- Fabric: about 45 x 35cm (18 x 14in)
- Lace: 36cm (14¼in) (for exterior)
- Lace: 40 cm (16in) (for interior)

To make
1 Copy the pattern piece (see page 51) on to the fabric
2 Cut two, adding a 5mm (¼in) seam allowance.
3 Sew the exterior lace to the right side of the lower (long) sides of the bag.

4 With right sides (RS) together, sew both pieces together between the purse frame markings.
5 Turn through to the right side.
6 Glue then sew the purse on to the frame.
7 Glue the interior lace trim around the inside of the frame to hide the stitches.

Capri sewing kit

Dimensions: 13 x 11cm (5 x 4½in)

For this project, you will need to know the size of the tape measure you plan to use.

Materials
- Purse frame: 9 x 4.5cm (3½ x 1¾in)
- Felt: 11 x 13cm (4½ x 5in)
- Floral fabric: 11 x 13cm (4¼ x 5in) + 4cm x 7cm (1½ x 2¾in) (amount required for a tape measure 5cm/2in) in diameter by 2cm /¾in).
- Lining fabric: 11 x 13cm (4¼ x 5in)
- Polyester interfacing: 1 circle same diameter as tape measure (here 5cm/2in) + 1 strip same circumference as tape measure 17 x 2cm (6¾ x ¾in).
- Wadding (batting): 10 x 10cm (4 x 4in)
- Soft toy filler to stuff the pincushion

To make
1 Trace the template on to the floral fabric (cut 1), felt (1), lining (2) and wadding (2). Add a 5mm (½in) seam allowance to all pieces, except the wadding, and cut out the number of pieces specified on the template.
2 Sew the strip and circle of polyester interfacing together using baseball stitch. Create an opening in the strip so that you can pull out the measuring tape.
3 Position the 4 x 7cm (1½ x 2¾in) piece of fabric on top of the tape measure, pull it taut and mark where the end of the measuring tape will emerge. Make a small opening, then edge it in buttonhole stitch to prevent the fabric from fraying when you use the measuring tape.
4 If you want to embroider the cover of the tape measure, do it now.
5 Pop the tape measure inside the polyester interfacing with the stop button at the top.
6 Gently pull out a short length of measuring tape and thread it through the opening in the polyester interfacing. Position the fabric cover on top. Matching the buttonhole to the opening in the polyester interfacing, thread the measuring tape through.
7 Stretch the floral fabric over the tape measure, keep it taut and slipstitch it around the edge of the polyester interfacing.
8 Sew the lace all around the edge of the tape measure cover.
9 With right sides (RS) together, sew the exterior fabric and felt together between the points indicated on the pattern piece for the purse frame. Turn through to the right side.
10 Stitch the cover of the tape measure to the front (felt side) of the purse.

11 With the lining pieces RS together, lay both pieces of wadding on one side of the lining. Stitch all the layers together between the points indicated for the purse frame.

12 Tuck the lining/wadding, wrong sides (WS) together, into the exterior section with the side with the wadding on it next to the floral fabric. Stuff a little bit of soft toy filler between the two pieces of wadding. The two layers will be:

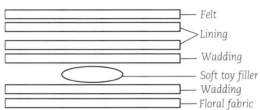

— Felt
— Lining
— Wadding
— Soft toy filler
— Wadding
— Floral fabric

13 Make a small turning along the top.

14 Glue (if the frame has no U-channel) and sew the purse frame into position.

Template for Capri travel sewing kit

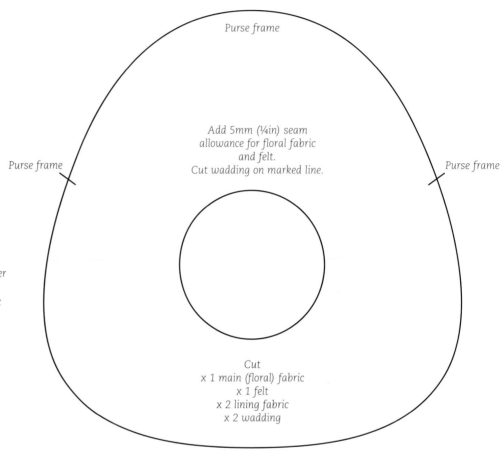

Purse frame

Purse frame

Purse frame

Add 5mm (¼in) seam allowance for floral fabric and felt.
Cut wadding on marked line.

Cut
x 1 main (floral) fabric
x 1 felt
x 2 lining fabric
x 2 wadding

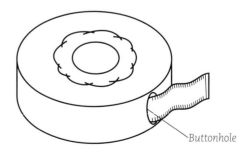

Buttonhole

Glasses or mobile phone case

Dimensions: 12 x 18.5cm (4¾ x 7¼in)

Materials
- Flex frame: 12 x 2cm (4¾ x ¾in)
- Exterior fabric: 48 x 26cm (19 x 10¼in)
- Lining: 36 x 24cm (14½ x 9½in)
- Ribbon: 1.50m (60in) long x 18mm (¾in) wide
- Lace: 1.5m x 14mm (60 x ½in)

To make

1 Cut two 12 x 23.5cm (4¾ x 9¼in) rectangles from your exterior fabric.

2 Cut two 12 x 18cm (4¾ x 7in) rectangles from your lining fabric.

3 With right sides (RS) together, sew the lining pieces together along the sides and base, taking a 1cm (³⁄₈in) seam allowance.

4 Make a narrow turning across the top edge of the lining towards the wrong side and press with a hot iron.

5 With RS together, sew the exterior fabric pieces together along the sides and base starting 5.5cm (2in) from the top.

6 Press the side seams open with a hot iron from top to bottom.

7 Create a 2.5cm (1in) flap across each side of the top and stitch it 5mm (¼in) from the bottom.

8 Turn the exterior fabric through to RS and tuck the lining inside still wrong sides (WS) out.

9 Sew the lining on to the lower edge of the flap with tiny slipstitches.

10 Insert the flex frame into the flaps.

11 Sew the lace on to the ribbon for the carrying strap.

12 Attach the two ends of the ribbon to the sides of the glasses case, as shown.

Dainty handbag

Dimensions: 22 x 22cm (9 x 9in)
(+ height of bag handle)

Materials
- Purse frame with metal carrying handle: 16 x 7cm (6¼ x 2¾in).
- Lace: 50cm (19½in)
- Exterior fabric: 55 x 45cm (22 x 18in)
- Lining fabric: 55 x 45cm (21½ x 17¾in)
- Fabric for inside pocket: 10 x 20cm (4 x 8in)
- Wadding (batting): 44 x 40cm (16½ x 15¾in)

To make
1 Trace the pattern pieces on to your exterior fabric, lining and batting. The pattern includes a 5mm (¼in) seam allowance.
2 Cut out the pieces.

Inside pocket
1 Fold the fabric for the inside pocket in two lengthways, with right sides (RS) facing. Sew together taking a 5mm (¼in) seam allowance and leaving an opening in one side. Turn the pocket RS out and press with a hot iron.
2 Sew the lace across the top of the inside pocket, turning under about 5mm (¼in) of lace on either side.
3 Centre the inside pocket on the RS of one piece of lining and stitch around three sides, leaving the top edge open.

Bag
1 Place the pieces of exterior fabric RS together and stitch between the points marked on the pattern piece for the purse frame. Turn RS out.
2 Repeat with the lining fabric, but leave this wrong sides (WS) facing.
3 Tuck the lining into the exterior body of the bag, then slip a piece of wadding down each side between the lining and the exterior fabric.
4 Stitch up the opening across the top of the bag, making a narrow fold and just catching the wadding in the seam line to keep it in place.
5 Stitch the lace around the top outside edges of the bag.
6 Sew on the purse frame.

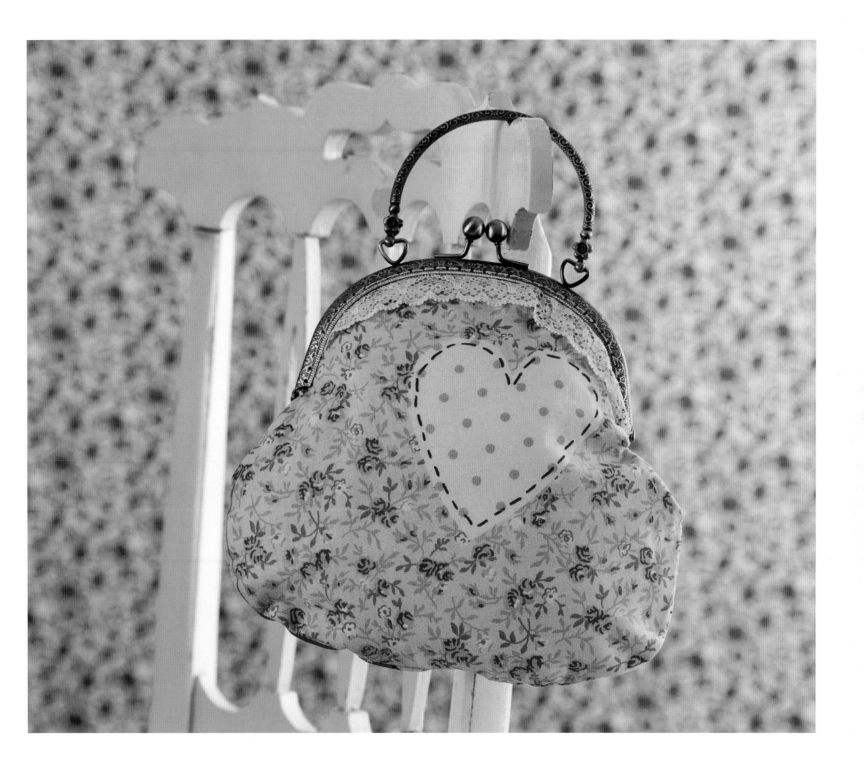

Template for Dainty handbag

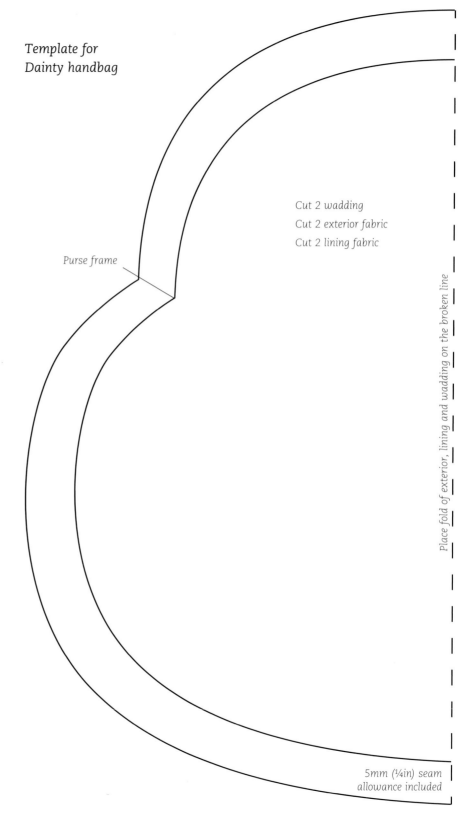

Purse frame

Cut 2 wadding
Cut 2 exterior fabric
Cut 2 lining fabric

Place fold of exterior, lining and wadding on the broken line

5mm (¼in) seam
allowance included

Templates for Floral coin purse

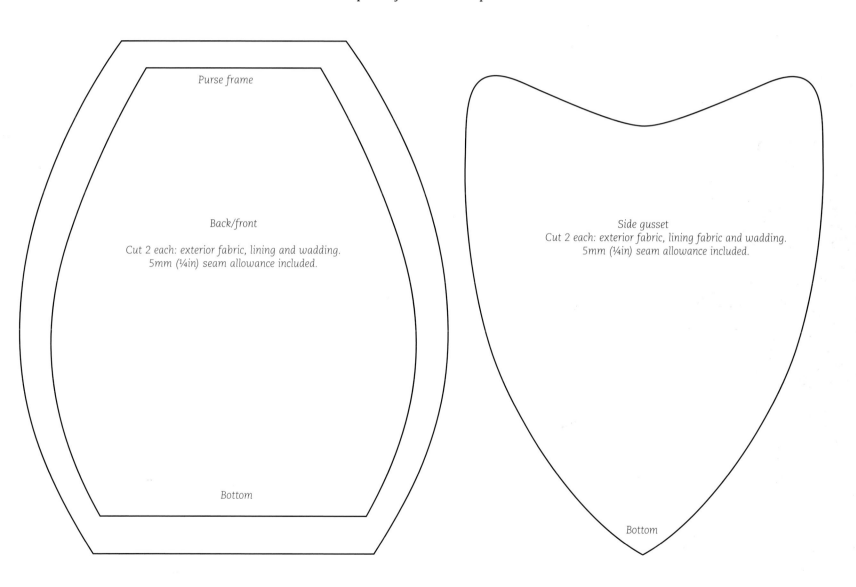

Purse frame

Back/front

Cut 2 each: exterior fabric, lining and wadding.
5mm (¼in) seam allowance included.

Bottom

Side gusset
Cut 2 each: exterior fabric, lining fabric and wadding.
5mm (¼in) seam allowance included.

Bottom

Floral coin purse

Dimensions: 10 x 12cm (4 x 4¾in)

Materials

- Purse frame: 8 x 5cm (3¼ x 2in)
- Floral fabric: 26 x 22cm (10¼ x 8¾in)
- Purple cotton: 16 x 22cm (6¼ x 8¾in)
- Lining fabric: 26 x 22cm (10¼ x 8¾in) + sides 16 x 22cm (6¼ x 8¾in)
- Double-sided fusible webbing: 26 x 22cm (10¼ x 8¾in) + sides 16 x 22cm (6¼ x 8¾in)
- Lightweight wadding (batting): 22 x 26cm (8¾in x 10¼in)

To make

1 Trace the front/back pattern piece (see page 65) twice on to the floral fabric, lining and wadding (seam allowance included). Trace the side gusset pattern piece twice on to the purple fabric, lining and wadding. Cut out the fusible webbing on the marked (sewing) line; you will need two front/back pieces and two sides gusset pieces.

2 Cut out all of the pieces.

3 Place the front and back pieces of exterior fabric right sides (RS) together and stitch across the bottom.

4 With RS together, sew the sides of the gusset to the front/back assembly. The lower tip of the side gusset should align with the front/back seam. The rounded dip at the top will be enclosed by the purse frame (see page 65).

5 Attach the fusible webbing to the wrong side (WS) of the lining.

6 Lay the wadding on the WS of lining (over the fusible webbing). Press the lining/wadding together with a hot iron under a piece of greaseproof paper to fuse them.

7 Repeat step 3 and 4 to assemble the lining/wadding purse.

8 With the RS of the lining to the WS of the floral body, tuck the lining into the purse.

9 Stitch together along the top edge leaving an opening so that you can turn your work RS out.

10 Sew the purse on the frame.

Panther coin purse

Dimensions: 13 x 12 cm (5 x 4¾in)

Materials
- 1 sheet self-adhesive fabric in grey polka dot
- 1 sheet self-adhesive fabric in panther print
- Purse frame: 8 x 4cm (3¼ x 1½in) (black)
- Fine lace: 24cm (9½in)
- Black linen thread

To make
1 Trace the outline of the pattern piece on to thin card or similar and cut out.
2 Cut two 14 x 15.5cm (5½ x 6¼in) rectangles from both sheets of self-adhesive fabric

   Note: this is slightly larger than the template, which includes a 5mm (¼in) seam allowance.
3 Carefully peel the paper off the back of the rectangles.
4 Lay the rectangle of grey polka dot fabric on a firm surface, sticky side up. Keeping it as flat as possible, press the sticky side of the rectangle of panther fabric on to it. You now have a grey spotted side and a panther side. Repeat with the other two rectangles.
5 Pin the template to each prepared rectangle in turn and cut out along the marked line.
6 Carefully glue or stitch the lace on to the grey polka dot fabric between the marks indicated for the purse frame on the pattern piece.
7 With right sides (RS) together, i.e. the panther fabric, sew the two halves of the coin purse together.
8 Turn RS out then sew on to the purse frame.

Template for the Panther coin purse

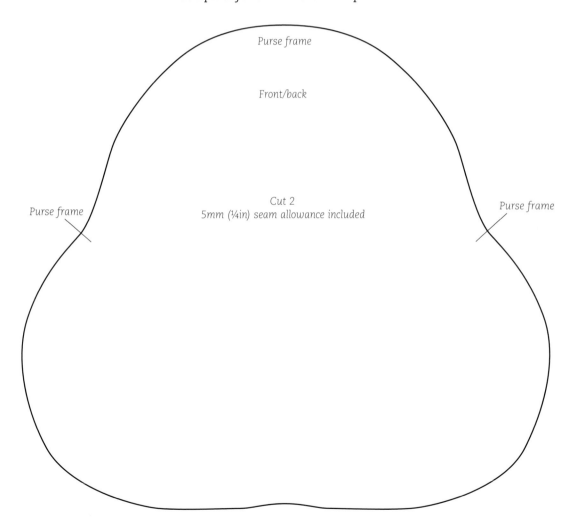

Purse frame

Front/back

Purse frame

Cut 2
5mm (¼in) seam allowance included

Purse frame

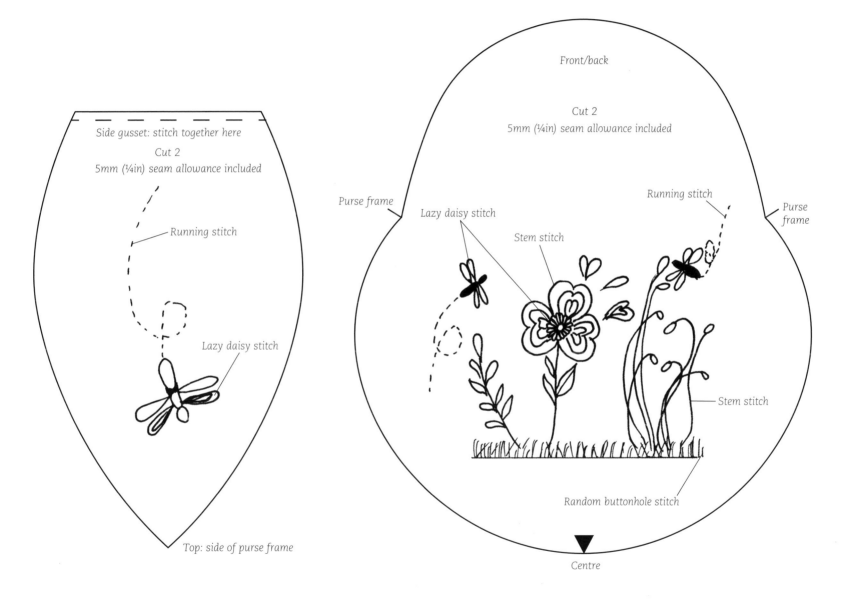

Embroidery motifs and templates for Wildflowers clutch purse

Side gusset: stitch together here

Cut 2

5mm (¼in) seam allowance included

Running stitch

Lazy daisy stitch

Top: side of purse frame

Front/back

Cut 2

5mm (¼in) seam allowance included

Purse frame

Lazy daisy stitch

Stem stitch

Running stitch

Purse frame

Stem stitch

Random buttonhole stitch

Centre

Wildflowers clutch purse

Dimensions: 10 x 12cm (4 x 4¾in)

Materials
- Purse frame: 8 x 5cm (3¼ x 2in)
- DMC embroidery threads: dark violet, medium violet, light violet, dark green, light green
- Plain green cotton or linen fabric: 24 x 28cm (9½ x 11in) + 7 x 24cm (2¾in x 8¼in) (side gussets)
- Lining fabric: 24 x 28cm (9½ x 11in) + 7 x 24cm (2¾in x 8¼in) (side gussets)
- Sheet of acetate film or tracing paper

To make
1 Transfer the embroidery design (see page 71) on to the green fabric.
2 Embroider the front of the purse and the two gusset pieces. Use two strands of embroidery thread and the stitches shown.
3 Copy the pattern pieces (see page 71) on to a sheet of rhodoid or tracing paper with a fine waterproof felt-tip pen.
4 Transfer both pattern pieces twice on to both the green fabric and the lining (a seam allowance is included).
5 Cut out the four pieces from the green fabric and the four from the lining fabric.
6 Place the green fabric side gusset piece right sides (RS) together and stitch along the broken line shown on the template. Press the seam open. Repeat with the lining side gusset pieces.
7 Place the green fabric gusset on the lining fabric gusset, RS together.
8 Use a pin to mark the centres of the front and back pieces.
9 With RS together, pin the gusset to the front of the purse and then to the back.
10 Now tack the front of the purse and the gusset together, starting from the middle and working to the left as far as the mark indicating the purse frame. Complete the other side to match, then repeat for the back of the purse.
11 Stitch firmly together and remove the tacking stitches.
12 Repeat with the lining fabric pieces.
13 With RS together, sew the green fabric to the lining, leaving an opening at the top to turn your work RS out.
14 Turn the purse RS out.
15 If you are using a sew-in purse frame with a U-channel, attach the purse (green fabric and lining).
16 If there is no U-channel, turn the top of the fabric over along the top, then sew it on to the purse frame.

Trendy gothic-print bag

Dimensions: 30 x 30cm (12 x 12in)

Materials
- Exterior fabric: Nightshade fabric (Vapor) by Tula Pink for Free Spirit (or similar fabric print): 70 x 80cm (28 x 32in)
- Lining fabric (optional): Nightshade fabric (Vapor) by Tula Pink for Free Spirit (or similar fabric print): 70 x 80cm (28 x 32in)
- Fabric for the sides: 30 x 80cm (12 x 32in)
- Glue-on purse frame: 22 x 7.5cm (8¾ x 3in)
- Bag handles: 56 cm (23in)
- Glue (for the purse frame)
- Double-sided fusible webbing: 70 x 80cm (28 x 32in)
- Wadding (batting): 70 x 80cm (28 x 32in)

To make
1 Trace each pattern piece twice on to the exterior fabric, lining, fusible webbing and wadding.

2 Cut out all pattern pieces. Note: 5mm (¼in) seam allowance included.

3 With right sides (RS) together, sew the two pieces of exterior fabric that make up the gusset (underside) of the bag.

4 With RS together, pin one edge of the gusset to the front of the bag and the other to the back.

5 Tack along the pinned sections, starting from the middle of the gusset and working to the left, finishing the line of tacking just below the mark for the purse frame on the pattern piece. Complete in same way on the other side, then repeat for the back.

6 Sew the handles on to the right side of the front and the back of the bag.

7 Stitch the tacked pieces together, then remove the tacking stitches.

8 Position the double-sided fusible webbing on top of the wadding and press down with a hot iron over a sheet of greaseproof paper.

9 Assemble the lining and wadding in the same order as the exterior fabric.

10 Position the wrong side (WS) of the lining (the side with the fusible webbing on it) on top of the wadding. Press down on the lining fabric with a hot iron to fuse it to the wadding.

11 With RS together, sew the exterior and lining fabrics together, leaving an opening in one side. Turn your bag RS out.

12 Slipstitch the opening closed.

13 Glue the bag into the purse frame.

Templates for Trendy gothic-print bag

base
Gusset (underside)
Cut 2
5mm (¼in) seam allowance included
Position fabric fold line here

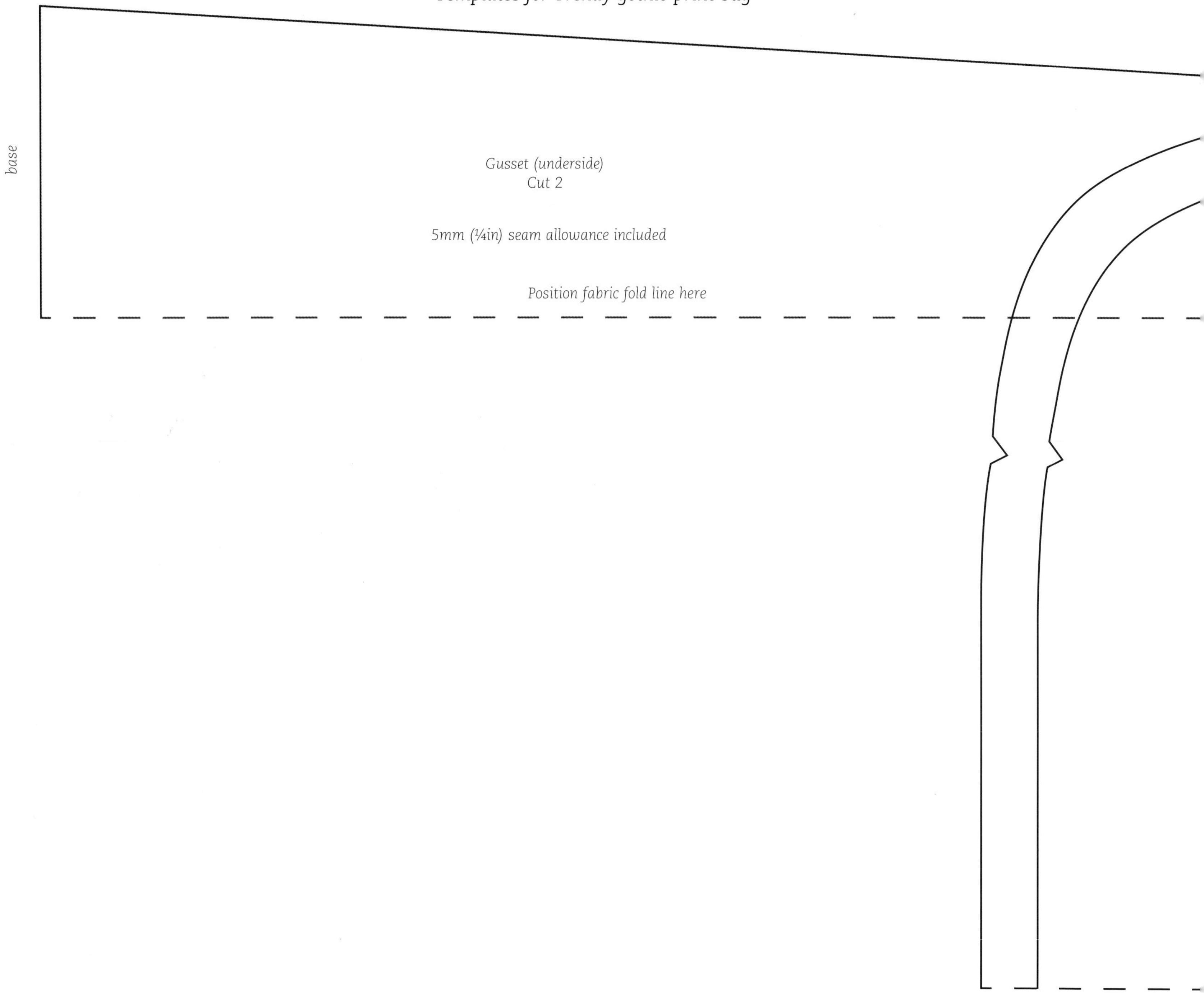

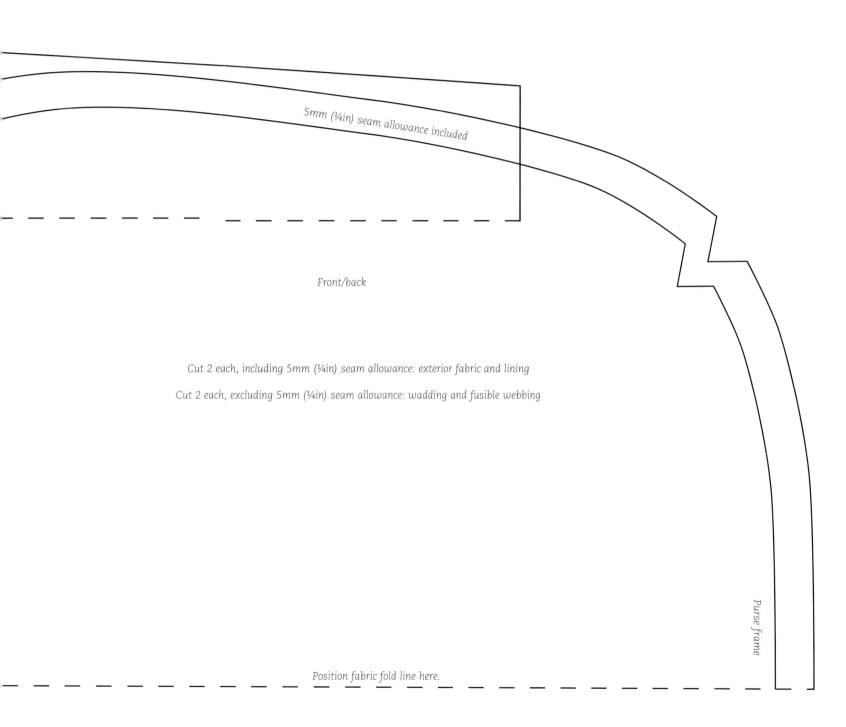

5mm (¼in) seam allowance included

Front/back

Cut 2 each, including 5mm (¼in) seam allowance: exterior fabric and lining

Cut 2 each, excluding 5mm (¼in) seam allowance: wadding and fusible webbing

Position fabric fold line here.

Purse frame